Hero Dog Stories 2

18 More True Stories

of Amazing Dogs

Jennifer Ogden

Table of Contents

__Introduction__

Dogs are truly man's best friend. They are there for you in the good times and the bad times. They make you smile and they also make you want to say a few choice words when they string garbage across the house or yard. As a dog owner, I have owned many different breeds over the years. They have all had very different personalities but all of them have held a special place in my heart.

I currently have a Bassett hound and a Chihuahua mix. They are complete opposites. Barney, the Bassett hound, is very loving and silly.

Cupcake, the Chihuahua mix, is very bratty but can also be very sweet when she wants to be. Cupcake does not like when Barney steals her attention. She will nip at his ears but Barney just ignores her and scoots on in besides me to get his much needed attention. Barney will stay next to me as long as I pet him. He is such a simple dog and he makes me laugh with those big old droopy eyes. Cupcake, on the other hand, lets me know when she is done with my affection. She simply gets up and goes to the other room to snuggle down in her pet bed.

Any dog lover knows that although a dog is not a human they still win a special spot within the family. I know Barney will sit at the back door every evening and bark until I give him his nightly treat. He likes to double dip! Sometimes my husband won't know I have given Barney his treat. Barney will bark at my husband until he gets one from him as well.

Cupcake always knows when its dinner time. She scouts the floor for crumbs and helps out with ingredients that hit the floor while I'm cooking. Needless to say, it probably wouldn't hurt her to lose a few pounds.

This is my second book about amazing, heroic dogs. I loved writing my first book, *Hero Dog Stories: 16 True Stories of Amazing Dogs,* and hearing stories from readers about their own special dogs.

I really believe that if I were in danger my dogs would come to the rescue. I guess you could say they are my inspiration for writing this book. I treat my dogs like family because deep inside I know they love me as much as I love them and, if and when I needed them, they would be heroes and rescue me and my family just like the heroic dogs in this book.

Please note that due to copyright issues I was unable to get pictures of the actual dogs mentioned in each story but I have done my best to provide pictures of the hero dog's breed so you can see what the hero dog looks like.

Wishing you and your own amazing dog friends the very best,

Jennifer

<u>Shelby</u>

Shelby is a 7 year-old German Shepard who has made her home in Ely, Iowa with the Walderbach family. It was wintertime in Iowa. The wind was blowing fiercely as the snow fell but for the Walderbachs life was quiet and peaceful. That changed on the evening of December 13. Earlier that day John and Janet Walderbach decided to keep their friend's children for the night. Their daughter Joleen who was Shelby's owner was not there but the house was filled with the sound of laughter as the children ran and played.

For John and Janet it had been a long day of baking Christmas cookies and having fun with their two young overnight visitors. John and Janet went to sleep soon after they put the children to bed. It seemed like no time at all before they were awakened by the cries of the children. Janet and John, along with the kids, were experiencing horrible stomachaches and bad headaches. Janet decided to rock the youngest child back to sleep. Shelby watched Janet closely as she was rocking the young child. Shelby could sense there was danger.

The rocking stopped. Shelby nudged Janet to wake her, but Janet didn't move. She had passed out. Shelby continued to whine and nudge Janet until she regained consciousness. Shelby then ran to John to alert him. John could tell that Shelby was very anxious. She had her ears down and her tail between her legs but she refused to leave the family's side.

John and Janet tried to make sense of what was causing their sickness.

John noticed how odd Shelby was acting so he let her outside, but this made Shelby even more anxious. She immediately began barking and scratching at the door frantically. Shelby realized the family needed to get out of the house and would not stop until everyone in the house joined her outside.

At that point, Janet and John made the decision to go to the hospital because there seemed to be something about the house that was making them very sick. Once they got to the hospital, the doctors diagnosed Janet, John, and the two children with carbon monoxide poisoning. They were immediately placed into a hyperbolic chamber to remove the carbon monoxide from their bodies and help prevent any damage. Their treatment was successful and they were soon released from the hospital, healthy and happy.

Doctors said that they were very fortunate to make it out of the home alive. When the Walderbach home was tested for carbon monoxide, the levels were measured at 280 parts per million. This is a deadly level of carbon monoxide. They could have died or suffered severe long-term damage to their health. Luckily, Shelby was there to make sure they all got out. Shelby saved her family. Shelby also survived from being exposed to the potentially deadly levels of carbon monoxide as well.

Shelby's heroic measures did not go unnoticed. She won the 45th Skippy dog hero of the year award. Shelby's owner, Joleen, received $500, a year's supply of Skippy brand dog food, and a Skippy Dog Hero food bowl that was engraved with Shelby's name. The Walderbachs are thankful to have Shelby in their family. This story could have been ended very tragically but Shelby was brave enough and smart enough to save the people she loves.

<u>Blue</u>

Australian Blue Heelers are known to be robust and hard working dogs. They are bred to work long hours herding various types of animals. They are also known for their loyalty. This description fits Ruth Gay's dog Blue perfectly.

85-year-old Ruth had decided to take her 2-year-old dog Blue for a walk before turning in for the night. It was almost 9:00 p.m. and darkness had fallen in Fort Myers, Florida. Ruth didn't mind walking in the dark because she knew that her dog Blue would protect her. Blue weighed in at 35-pounds but he was very protective and loyal to Ruth.

As they walked back toward their home Ruth slipped on some wet grass. Ruth was hurt pretty badly. Her shoulder was dislocated and her nose was broken. She rolled to her back and started screaming for help. Ruth shared a home with her daughter and son in-law but they were out for the evening. Now the darkness of the evening became a problem for Ruth. She fell in a spot not easily seen so if someone did pass nearby they wouldn't see her.

Blue stayed by her side. Although Ruth knew the situation was serious, she didn't realize just how serious until Blue started growling. Ruth realized she was in true danger. Blue was growling uncontrollably and even left Ruth's side which was not something Blue would typically do. Ruth heard the sounds of Blue fighting. She couldn't see what Blue was fighting with but she could tell by Blue's demeanor that he was fighting with something.

Blue began yelping and whining and Ruth realized that he was in pain and suffering from injuries. Everything went quiet. This worried Ruth even more than her own injuries. Had the predator gotten the best of Blue? Ruth lay in the dark battered and bruised thinking that her beloved Blue was dead. Now all she could do was wait for her daughter to come home and hope whatever Blue fought with didn't return.

An hour passed, then Ruth heard a car pull into the driveway. She was so thankful that her long wait in the darkness was over but what happened next made her even more thankful. Blue greeted Ruth's daughter Sylvia in the driveway and started barking uncontrollably. He led Sylvia and her husband Albert to Ruth. Ruth greeted them happily and told them she thought Blue was dead.

Sylvia and Albert took Ruth to the hospital where she had one shoulder reset and the other operated on. Blue was taken to the vet where he was treated for multiple puncture wounds. Both of them were very sore but they managed to live through this traumatic event.

What was the predator that Blue fought off? It was an alligator!

Earlier that day Ruth saw three alligators in the canal close to their home. This was only 50 feet from where Ruth laid battered and bruised. Blue had fought one of the alligators and won. Although Blue sustained injuries during the fight, he managed to scare the gator away. That very gator showed up days later close to Ruth's house with a torn up snout. Blue might have gotten hurt but the alligator knew Blue meant business.

Blue was given an award for his bravery. Ruth and her family feel very blessed to have Blue in their family. If Blue had not reacted quickly to the alligator, Ruth could have suffered deadly injuries. Thanks to Blue, Ruth was not touched by the alligator. Ruth and Blue both made full recoveries.

Kankuntu

Peter and Betty Lee from Manchester, UK were no strangers to the sea. They were on a voyage around the world aboard their yacht *Raven Eye*. Their family dog Kankuntu, a mixed-breed, was with them. It was a beautiful day for sailing as they head to the Caribbean. The breeze was blowing and the sun was shining.

Everything suddenly changed when a boat approached their yacht. At first, they thought that it was a fishing boat so they were not alarmed. Then, shots were fired from the boat! Desperate to get away, Peter rammed the boat with his yacht knocking down the leader of the five pirates. One of the pirates fired directly at Peter but missed. At that moment, Peter realized that there was nothing more to do but to surrender.

The pirates made their way on board and tied the hands of the Lees. Kankuntu lunged at the assailants desperately trying to fight them off and protect her family. Sadly, Kankuntu was no match for the pirates' guns and knives. She was shot and stabbed and left in a corner, fighting for her life. The couple could not believe this was happening to them. They had sailed the sea many times and never in any way, felt threatened. This time, their lives were at stake.

Peter's hands and feet were tied. His face was on the ground and a pistol was pointed at his head. His wife was with two of the pirates who were demanding money. She was held at gunpoint as well. Their dog Kankuntu lay in a pool of blood because she had fought, trying to protect her family from the bandits. The pirates demanded money and became increasingly angry when they found out that the couple only had a few hundred dollars aboard. They fought to get Betty's wedding ring from her finger but she would not give it up.

After what felt like an eternity, the bandits gave up and escaped using their own boat. The couple felt relieved that they escaped this frightening ordeal alive. How about their brave dog Kankuntu? The dog was fighting for her life. It took several days, but thankfully, she made a full recovery. The veterinarian was able to retrieve the bullet from Kankuntu.

After the incident, Peter realized just how brave Kankuntu had been. For him, Kankuntu was like a lion, a very brave animal who does not easily give up. As for Peter and Betty, they have no plans on letting this ordeal slow them down. They plan to continue their voyage around the world. They coordinated with the local authorities to locate the pirates so that nobody else will experience what they have to go through. Because of this, they now they take more precautions, but one thing remains, Kankuntu will always be with them on their journeys.

<u>Junior</u>

Dogs come in all shapes and sizes. No matter what the size of the dog is, there is always a certain level of loyalty to its owner. Junior is a poodle mixed breed who found his home in Fort Lauderdale, Florida with the Davilmar family. Junior may be a small dog, but he is hailed as a hero for saving his family.

It was early in the morning when Madelus Davilmar woke up from the continuous barking of his four-legged friend Junior. Once Madelus got out of bed, he realized that the house was on fire! The smoke alarm was blaring in the house. He then realized the severity of the scene. There were eight people in the house. All of them had heard the smoke detector except for Madelus. He somehow had slept through it.

The house was filled with heavy smoke. Madelus had to feel his way out. Once outside, he was joined by his family and faithful dog Junior. Firefighters arrived on the scene to put out the blazing fire. Had it not been for Junior, Madelus might have died that night.

The fire was said to be electrical in origin and started in a guest bedroom. The home was severely damaged, but thanks to Junior all eight people escaped without harm. Junior did not stop barking until everyone was outside. It is because of his bravery the family made it out safely.

Belle

Belle started her life like some other dogs do. She waited for a home in a pet store. She was actually purchased twice but given back each time by dissatisfied buyers. To be clear, nothing was wrong with her, she was a cute and perky beagle pup who just had not found the right home yet.

Kevin Weaver, 34, of Ocoee, Florida, happened to be in the market for a dog. One of his friends mentioned seeing Belle in the window of the pet store. Weaver went to check her out the next day. He instantly fell in love with her. He told the storeowner to pack her up because he was taking her home.

Belle didn't possess any special skills, but she was a great companion for Kevin. As time went by, Kevin's diabetes worsened and he started to develop seizures. He was often worried about his condition because he could slip into a coma and never wake up. Something had to be done but he wasn't sure what.

Kevin was working as a flight attendant at the time. His diabetes had worsened and while on a flight, one of his passengers, who traveled often, suggested that he get Belle special training as a medical assistance dog. Kevin thought about it for a while and realized the training could save his life.

The question was: could Belle be trained to do what Kevin needed?

The training was not cheap. The training fee was $9,000 and it took a total of nine months of intensive schooling. Belle turned out to be a great student.

Belle's training taught Belle to lick Kevin's nostrils to smell the ketone level on his breath. Beagles have a very keen sense of smell. It is hundreds of times as strong as a human's sense of smell. If Kevin's ketone level became too high, he could slip into a coma and possibly die.

Also, Belle learned to paw at Kevin's leg to warn him that his sugar levels are out of range. This warning could prevent Kevin from having a seizure and slipping into a coma. If Kevin were to pass out or have a seizure, Belle was taught to get her owner's cell phone and hold down on the number 9, which was programmed for 911. Kevin wondered if a dog would be able to complete all of the actions needed to get him help and to do so without panicking. Most adults would panic in a situation like this.

Everyone hoped that Belle's training would never have to be put to the test in real life, but just eight months after Belle had completed her training it was. Kevin woke up that morning feeling as if it was just any other day. He did feel dizzy and slightly nauseated, but not enough to cause him to worry about it. Belle, however, could sense a problem. She began pawing at Kevin's leg and whining uncontrollably. This wasn't Belle's normal behavior, but he thought that she just needed to pee. She placed her leash on her to take her out.

That was all Kevin could remember. He collapsed on the kitchen floor with a seizure. This was the first seizure he had since Belle had completed her training. Belle reacted quickly and put into action what she learned in the training. As 34-year-old Kevin lay unconscious on the floor, Belle fetched his cell phone and pressed down the number 9 that would automatically call 911. Dispatchers could hear nothing in the background except for barking. It was enough for them to know someone needed help.

When a rescue team arrived, they found Kevin still unconscious on the floor and Belle right by his side. Belle was brought to the hospital with Kevin so she could be by his side when he regained consciousness. Hours later, Kevin woke and found Belle right by his side. Kevin's roommate did not

41

return to the house until 5 hours after Kevin's seizure. If Belle had not been there to make the life-saving call to 911, this story would have had a very tragic ending. Kevin would have slipped into a coma due to a dangerously low blood sugar level.

Kevin was very thankful of his decision to enroll Belle in the training that saved his life. Belle has a very special place in Kevin's heart. He knew from the day he saw her in the pet store that she was special and loyal.

Kevin was treated and released from the hospital. On his way home, he stopped at a steakhouse and celebrated by buying a steak dinner for Belle and himself. Kevin was forced to give up his job as a flight attendant due to his seizures. Despite this setback, he still believed that every cloud has a silver lining. He was able to get a job at Walt Disney World. They even gave him an office job where he could bring Belle. Every day at work, Belle is right by Kevin's side. She wears a vest to show that she is a medical assistance dog and lays at his feet as he works.

Not only is she a hero in Kevin's book, she has also been nationally recognized for her heroism. Normally, a dog would be forced to ride in the cargo portion of the plane, but not Belle. She rode a plane to Washington in a first class seat along with Kevin. She was nominated by Cingular wireless for the VITA Wireless Samaritan Award presented by the CTIA Wireless Foundation. This foundation recognizes heroes who use their cell phones to stop crimes, save a life, or help during an emergency. Belle was the first dog to win this award. Kevin is certain that Belle loves

him and that she is his best friend.

<u>Toby</u>

We all know the saying that a dog is man's best friend. In some cases, this shines through more than others. Toby is a perfect example. He really is his owner's best friend. Toby is a 2-year-old golden retriever. His owner is 45-year-old jewelry artist Debbie Parkhurst.

Debbie and Toby live in Calvert, Maryland. Toby is full of life and has brought Debbie so much joy. It was a Friday afternoon and Debbie was home alone with Toby. She was enjoying her day and decided to fix a snack for herself. She sliced an apple and began eating it.

Without warning, one of the apple slices became stuck in Debbie's windpipe. She reacted quickly by throwing her body against a chair to try to dislodge the apple. It didn't work, so she began pounding her chest with her fist. This alerted Toby that there was a problem. Toby sprang into action by placing his front paws on Debbie's shoulders to push her to the ground. Once she was on the ground, he began jumping up and down on her chest.

Finally, the apple managed to break loose and Toby kept Debbie awake by licking her face. In fact, Debbie had paw-print shaped bruises on her chest from where Toby performed the Heimlich maneuver. A friend drove Debbie to the doctor, but she was only a little bruised and had a sore throat. Debbie was very thankful that her four-legged friend, Toby, was there to save her life!

<u>Shana</u>

Rescuing animals can be a very rewarding job. Eve and Norman Fetig have spent most of their life together rescuing animals. So when they had a chance to rescue a two-week-old half wolf, half German shepherd puppy, they did. A breeder had the pup and she was very sick. She required more attention than the breeder could give. The Fertigs took her willingly and named her Shana.

Eve and Norman fell in love with Shana. She was a loyal companion. Seven years had passed since they nursed her back to health. Shana had developed into a very big and muscular animal. She weighed about 160 pounds, the weight of many adult men.

The Fertigs didn't know that Shana would one day repay them for saving her life. It was a blustery day in October when the Fertigs were out scouting their property in Albany, New York for injured animals. They were both 81, but they refused to give up caring for the animals they love. They had a forest sanctuary set up where they kept and cared for wounded animals.

The couple was caring for a crow that had been shot blind in one of its eyes and had two broken legs. The couple had a routine of caring for the animals around 7 p.m. every evening. While in their forest sanctuary treating the crow, one of their lights went out. Knowing something must have happened Norman and Eve went outside to find the problem.

Without warning, large trees started falling down all around them blocking their path to their home and the other buildings they used for treating their rescued animals. A terrible snowstorm had hit New York and the Fertigs knew they were in trouble. The couple huddled in an alley between the buildings where they would be protected from the falling trees.

Neither of them could safely climb over the trees, nor had they dressed for the drastic drop in temperature. Hours earlier, it had been a crisp fall day but that had all changed. The Fertigs huddled together to try to stay warm. It was now 9:30 p.m. and both of them feared they wouldn't be found for days.

Fear had set in for Eve and all she could think was that they were trapped with no way out. That's when Shana sprang into action. She began to dig beneath the fallen trees. Shana went everywhere Norman and Eve went. Today, Eve was feeling very blessed to have Shana with them. Shana dug through the snow with her teeth and claws making a tunnel. As she went along, she was barking as if to tell the Fertigs to follow her.

It was now around 11:30 p.m. and Shana had successfully tunneled her way all the way to the Fertigs home. She came back to where Eve was and grabbed Eve's jacket sleeves in her mouth. Shana managed to maneuver Eve onto Shana's back and drag Eve into the tunnel. Norman held onto Eve's legs and Shana dragged the couple through the tunnel of snow she had made. Shana dragged them through the tunnel to the house. With Shana's help, the Fertigs arrived home at 2 a.m.

They fell into their door and lay upon the floor, thankful to be alive and out of the extreme conditions of the snowstorm just outside their door. There was no heat or electricity in their home. Neighbors had been concerned about the couple because they could not reach them by telephone so they contacted the local fire department who showed up at the Fertigs' home the next morning. Exhausted from the events that occurred, Norman and Eve had not moved an inch from where they had dropped to on the floor the night before.

The fireman urged the Fertigs to take shelter at the firehouse with others in the community who had lost electricity, but the Fertigs were not happy about this because they were told that they would have to leave Shana behind. The fireman warned the couple that it would probably take days before power will be restored, but the Fertigs remained in their home with Shana. They had no hot water, heat or electricity but they survived. Shana slept with the couple to keep them warm. During the days without electricity, the firemen brought them water and food.

People couldn't believe the tunnel that Shana had dug for the Fertigs. When they saw how long it was they understood why the Fertigs refused to leave her. She had saved their lives and was a true hero. Finally, the firehouse had cleared out enough that the Fertigs were allowed to bring Shana with them. Shana was hailed as a hero by the firemen and treated like one as well.

Shana was awarded the Citizens for Humane Animal Treatment's Hero's Award. This award is normally given to people, but it was awarded to

Shana for the extreme bravery that she showed for

her owners, Norman and Eve. She was given a

plaque with her picture on it. It hangs in the Fertigs'

living room today. Shana showed her loyalty and love

for her owners in a very brave way. She is more than

a pet, she is part of the family.

<u>Zoey</u>

Good things come in small packages. This is very true when talking about a small Chihuahua named Zoey. Denise and Monty Long own four dogs including Zoey. The dog may be the smallest, but she is also the biggest hero in Masonville, Colorado.

Denise and Monty were enjoying a warm, sunny day with their grandson Brooker in the back yard. One-year-old Brooker was splashing in a birdbath nearby while Zoey was also there watching as a snake made its way towards the child ready to strike. The dog wasted no time placing herself between the snake and Brooker.

Denise and Monty heard Zoey yelp and turned to see what happened. They saw the rattlesnake coiled up and ready to strike again. Monty quickly grabbed Brooker out of harm's way. The snake had missed Brooker, but Zoey was now suffering from a snakebite in the head. Monty was very shaken up by what could have happened. They were so thankful their dog saved Brooker's life.

Weighing only 5-pounds, Zoey required treatment quickly. Zoey was rushed to a veterinarian who began treatment right away. The treatment included plasma, morphine and anti-venom treatments. Zoey's head swelled up to the size of a large grapefruit. The only thing visible on Zoey's face was her little button nose. The snakebite left a large vertical scar on Zoeys's head and she nearly lost an eye.

Luckily, Zoey responded well to the treatment she was given and she was back playing with her family within a few days. The Longs are so thankful for their little dog and her very large heroic deed that saved their grandson.

<u>Juliana</u>

During September 1940-May 1941, Great Britain experienced many terrifying bombings known as the Blitz. During the Blitz, explosive bombs were dropped in more than 16 British cities. London was bombed 71 times during a raid that lasted for 57 straight nights. People all around London were very scared. They didn't know when the next bomb would drop or where it would land.

It was 1941 and a shopkeeper was in his home along with his trusted companion Juliana. Juliana was a well-behaved Great Dane. Without warning, one of the bombs from the Blitz fell onto the shopkeeper's roof and into his home! Juliana was very quick to run to the bomb and hike her leg. How she knew to urinate on the bomb to keep it from exploding was amazing in itself but she had saved her home from being blown up. For that, her owner was very thankful. Her actions earned her a Blue Cross Medal.

Three years later, Juliana demonstrated her heroism again. She warned customers of a fire that was ripping through her owner's shoe shop. Once again, she was awarded with a Blue Cross Medal for her bravery.

This story would have been lost to time and no one would have known of Juliana's bravery if not for an auctioneer who discovered it while doing a sweep of a home in Bristol. The second medal was found along with a photo of Juliana. There was also a plaque with the photo that reads: *Juliana - awarded a medal for extinguishing an incendiary bomb April*

1941. Awarded another for alerting the occupants of her master's burning shop November 1944.

The auctioneer admitted he often found treasures during house clearings. At the auction, Juliana's medal and portrait sold for 18 times more than the pre-sale estimate.

Sadly, Juliana did not have a happy ending to her life. She was given poison through her owner's letterbox located in the door. She died in 1945.

Amazingly, her heroic deeds will live on forever with the unveiling of her medals. What a fantastic story about a very brave dog. It could have been forgotten forever had the auctioneer not stumbled upon her plaque and the medal that told of her heroic deeds.

<u>Wheeler</u>

Dogs have long been valuable to society as more than family pets. They have been used as companions, served in the armed forces, and even lead blind people. This next story is about a dog named Wheeler. He is a police dog.

Wheeler is a 10-year-old German Shepherded who was rescued from the streets of Brooklyn and taken to an animal shelter. One of the rescue workers saw something special in him. Wheeler is very alert and has an amazing, protective nature. The rescue worker, recommend the dog to the New York State Police. Wheeler underwent a 20-week canine training program. After completing the program, he was paired with Trooper Michael Boburka.

Trooper Boburka enjoyed working with Wheeler. In fact, Trooper Boburka says Wheeler is one of the best dogs he has ever worked with. Wheeler makes it easy for his K-9 handler. They have a great partnership.

The canine unit division was launched in 1975. At that time, there were only 3 dogs on the force. The police trained the dogs for the 1980 Winter Olympic Games in Lake Placid, New York. The dogs were trained to detect explosives. They were very great assets to the police force. Because of the success, the program grew and it is now comprised of 66 canine units. It includes 31 explosive detection teams, 32 narcotic detection teams and 3 teams of bloodhounds. Some dogs, like Wheeler, are cross trained as cadaver dogs which means they are able to locate dead bodies.

In Binghamton, New York, Wheeler is known as Sgt. Harry J. Wheeler. He is known as one of the best dogs on the task force. He has brought justice for many victims some of which would not have gotten justice had he not done his job. In the eight years that Wheeler has been with Trooper Boburka, Wheeler has located six missing bodies, uncovered dozens of drug stashes and located criminals hiding from the police. With all the tasks given to Wheeler, he is really a hero dog.

<u>Boydy</u>

Herbert Schutz, 76 years of age, had always considered his dog Boydy a loyal companion. Herbert and Boydy lived on a farm in rural Australia. Boydy, a sheepdog, always went with Herbert on his daily trips around his land. The farm is nestled at the bottom of an Australian mountain range. Life for them was quite simple. They had a few neighbors who would visit from time to time, but Herbert and Boydy were used to not seeing anyone for days.

One day, while checking on his farm, Herbert hit a tree. He managed to escape his four-wheel drive vehicle, but as he was exiting, the car rolled over on him. He was now pinned underneath his car in a very remote part of Australia. The chance of anyone finding him was very slim.

Luckily, he had Boydy with him. Boydy knew just what to do to help keep his owner alive. Sheepdogs have lots of fur. Boydy used that to his advantage to save his owner's life. He cuddled up next to Herbert to help keep him warm.

Herbert was in a lot of pain. Not only was he fighting the frigid temperatures, he was also suffering from a fractured skull, two broken hips and a dislocated shoulder. Herbert lay cold, hungry and severely injured with no one else by his side except for his loyal companion Boydy. He was in this condition for four days.

Herbert's daughter called his neighbors when she was unable to reach her father after several days. The neighbors couldn't find Herbert at his house so they decided to search for him. The search party saw his car, but didn't see anyone in it. As they were approaching the car, Boydy leaped to greet them. Boydy lead the search party to Herbert and they worked quickly to try to free Herbert from the wreckage.

Herbert was rushed to the hospital and treated for his injuries. He survived the four-day ordeal, all thanks to Boydy. When Herbert arrived at the hospital, he was covered in dog hair. This was a significant sign that Boydy stayed right by his side the whole time and kept him warm. Temperatures got as low as four degrees. If Boydy was not there to offer his body heat, Herbert likely would have died. Boydy is a true hero.

<u>Hachiko</u>

This next story is not really about a heroic dog, but it displays the incredible loyalty a dog has for its owner. Akitas are known to display loyalty to their owners. If an Akita is forced to find a new owner, they often have a very hard time readjusting. Some never do, and that is the case with Hachiko.

Dr. Ueno lived in the beautiful land of Japan. He taught at the Imperial University and lived a simple life. One day, he decided to adopt a companion. He brought home a two-month old Akita and named him Hachiko. Hachiko's fur was brilliant white and he grew to weigh over 90 pounds within the next year. Dr. Ueno and Hachiko became very close. They were always together.

Every morning, Hachiko walked his owner to the Shibuya train station and was there to greet him when he came home. They would walk home together and enjoy the rest of the evening.

On one memorable day, Hachiko had walked the professor to the train station that morning as he did every day. When Hachiko returned that evening, Dr. Ueno was not there. Hachiko waited, but his owner never showed up. Dr. Ueno suffered a stroke that day and died.

Every day after that Hachiko would come to the station looking for Dr. Ueno. After a while, Hachiko was sent to another part of Japan to live with Dr. Ueno's next of kin. He did not adjust well. People thought that because he was only owned by the professor for a year, he would be able to adjust to having a new family; however, Hachiko escaped his new home and returned to the train station to wait for his owner.

Since Hachiko wanted to stay close to the train station, the family decided to give him to Dr. Ueno's old gardener who lived nearby. Each day Hachiko would go to the train station at 6pm and wait for Dr. Ueno. Every evening Hachiko left that station filled with sorrow because his owner never showed up. Those who used the train each day recognized Hachiko and they were touched by his loyalty to Dr. Ueno. They would shower Hachiko with love and bring him food as well. Months turned into years and still Hachiko continued to wait for Dr. Ueno at the train station. Soon, he became a Japanese celebrity. They even made a statue in his honor and placed it at Shibuya station. It just so happened that Hachiko was there to celebrate his statue when they placed it.

Hachiko lived as a stray because he would not stay with anyone. He ate scraps and the food people would share with him; however, he also had to defend himself against other animals. He got very ill and the people admired Hachiko so much they paid his vet bill.

After many years, Hachiko was not the dog he once was. He was old and scarred up. Finally, ten years after his master's death, Hachiko was found in the streets of Shibuya, dead. People were filled with sorrow, but also found comfort in the fact that Hachiko could finally be with his beloved, Dr. Ueno.

To remember Hachiko's loyalty, a ceremony is held every year in his honor. There was also a movie made in his honor. His loyalty has been an inspiration for people all over the world for generations. Hachiko will never be forgotten.

<u>Gage</u>

The day started out like any other day. Bruce Lamb, a 52 years old, New Zealand constable had arrived at work with his loyal K-9 police dog named Gage. Bruce and Gage had been partners for some time. Both were accustomed to working with one another. Gage is a German shepherd and has always shown loyalty to his handler. In police work, loyalty is vital. Partners look out for each other. It's how they can be successful at their jobs.

Bruce's Sergeant called for backup at what Bruce thought would be a low-key crime scene. While one man was being arrested for drugs, another man had disappeared inside his house. Bruce was to go inside and get the man for questioning.

Bruce had no idea that Christopher Smith, the man inside the home, was armed and dangerous. Although Bruce didn't know it at the time, Christopher had no intention of giving up without a fight.

The plan was for Bruce and Gage to gain entry to the room where Christopher was hiding and to bring him outside. When the door was opened, Christopher was standing on a bed with a rifle pointed at Bruce. Christopher fired. The bullet ripped through Bruce's bottom lip and exited out the side of his jaw.

Bruce was now on the ground helpless and in pain. Christopher quickly took aim at Bruce once again. Christopher's intention was to finish Bruce off, but Gage leapt into action. Just as Christopher fired the second shot, Gage leaped over Bruce to protect him and to attack Christopher.

Christopher quickly escaped out a window. Bruce ran out of the house to get help then realized that Gage, who was still attached to his leash, was dead. Gage had taken the second bullet fired by Christopher and saved Bruce's life. Gage had been Bruce's loyal companion until the very end. Gage gave his life to protect Bruce.

Bruce will never forget what Gage did for him and will always honor and treasure the time they had together.

Bruce was only in the hospital for 2 days but did not return to his job for six months. It took several surgeries to repair his jaw. Christopher Smith was arrested soon after he shot Bruce and Gage and sentenced to 14 years in prison without the chance of parole.

When Bruce returned to work, he spent the first three months training his new partner, Mylo. Mylo is a black Labrador trained to find narcotics. Bruce now enforces search warrants with Mylo.

Although Bruce has a new partner, Bruce will never forget Gage or his heroic action. Gage's name was added to the list of 22 other animal heroes who have received the PDSA Gold Medal award and a medal was presented to Bruce.

Gage has his own Facebook page – RIP Gage the Police Dog.

<u>Vicious</u>

A 12-year-old Border Collie/Labrador mix named Vicious from Trial, British Columbia was relaxing at home with her owner Angie Prime. Don't let Vicious' name fool you. Although her name was Vicious, she was not mean at all. Angie always said Vicious was a 'cream puff' and very sweet.

Angie often left her sliding glass door open so that Vicious and two small puppies Angie had could go out to the back yard. Although it was starting to get dark, Angie kept the outside lights off so no bugs would come in the open door.

Vicious was lying at one end of the couch while Angie was at the other end. Angie was finishing a conversation with her husband when something caught her eye.

Angie turned to see what it was and came face-to-face with a cougar! Angie was helpless because there was no way of escaping the cougar. The cougar bunched his muscles to attack. In an effort to protect herself, Angie threw her arms up to protect her face. As the cougar leapt to attack, Angie let out a blood-curdling scream. Vicious wasted no time because she knew there was danger. She launched herself at the cougar. Luckily, the cougar was not willing to fight with Vicious. It quickly made an exit out the open door.

Vicious ran after the cougar through the back door. She wanted to make sure the beast was gone for good. Amazingly, Vicious returned to Angie unharmed.

Angie only had three puncture marks on her thigh where the cougar had swung at her. When officers arrived, they were sure that this story would have had a very different and far worse ending if not for Vicious. If Vicious had not reacted so quickly to scare the cougar away, Angie would likely have been seriously injured and possibly killed.

The Purina Animal Hall of Fame heard about Vicious' story and decided she was worthy of being inducted into their hall of fame. The cougar was later tracked down and euthanized. Animal Control Officials believe the cougar was starving and had entered Angie's home in search of food. Angie considers herself very lucky. She no longer leaves her back door open. Angie hails her trusty dog as a

hero and is very thankful she was there to protect her.

<u>Tatiana</u>

Service dogs are trained to be obedient and loyal to their owners. Their service makes their owner's life easier and safer. These dogs go through months of training and must pass many vigorous tests before being released to work for the owner. One may wonder why it is so important that the service dog pass a test before working for their owner. A service dog must always be ready and willing to do whatever it is to help their owner, and in many cases, even save their owner's life.

Christina Saint-Blancard had suffered from a hearing impairment as well as severe asthma for many years. She would wake in the middle of the night struggling for air. Despite her difficulties, she had managed to graduate from Iowa State University and was beginning to work on her master's degree. Unfortunately, Christina's health became worse and she had to return to her parents' home in Plantation, Florida.

Christina decided to get a service dog to assist her. That is when she found Tatiana. Tatiana was a beautiful Labrador who showed all of the traits necessary for a hearing service dog. She had been bred by the Orlando-based Canine Companions for Independence. Tatiana spent two years in California undergoing special training. After Tatiana was designated as Christina's service dog, Tatiana began to be trained to tell when Christina was having an asthma attack and get help.

Christina and her mom knew that Tatiana was not allowed to sleep with Christina until Tatiana had passed all of her training tests. One night Christina's mom agreed to allow Tatiana to sleep with Christina even though Tatiana had not yet passed her tests. Tatiana had been with Christina for two months now. She was excited to finally get the opportunity to snuggle up next to Tatiana.

Very early the next morning Christina woke up breathless. She couldn't talk or even make a sound. Fortunately, Tatiana was by her side and realized the urgency of the situation. Tatiana tried to rouse Christina but received no response. Tatiana quickly made her way down the dark hallway and into Christina's mother's room. Tatiana nudged Teresa, Christina's mom, with her nose and woke her up.

Teresa wasted no time because she knew that if Tatiana was waking her up there was a problem.

Paramedics later told Teresa it was a good thing that Tatiana was there. If the paramedics had not been alerted by Teresa and responded so quickly, Christina would have died. Teresa is so thankful Tatiana was there to save her daughter. It was lucky that she allowed Tatiana to sleep with Christina that night.

Tatiana is not only a hero to Christina and Teresa. She was given the Hero Dog Award in the American Humane Association's second annual competition.

This story is a testament that everything happens for a reason. The answers are sometimes not clear, but one thing is sure: Christiana feels very blessed to have Tatiana by her side. Tatiana is a loyal and trusted friend that saved Christina's life.

Hunter

Reyna Zurita lives in a quiet neighborhood with her hound dog Hunter. Reyna had adopted Hunter just three weeks before. He was 2-years-old and a perfect match for Reyna from the very beginning. She enjoyed the spirit of her hound. He was very loving and loyal.

Hunter always greeted Reyna at the door when she returned home, but on this particular day, he didn't greet her. Instead, he bolted straight out the door. This was not like him at all, so Reyna followed behind him to see what had him so upset. As Hunter left the yard and raced down the street, Reyna called for Hunter to stop, but he did not. He continued making his way down the street. Reyna was puzzled. She couldn't understand what Hunter was doing.

Hunter finally stopped about a half mile from Reyna's home. He stopped right in front of an infant laying still and unmoving on the ground. Reyna quickly grabbed the infant and started CPR. The baby was not breathing and was turning purple. The mother of the baby had placed him on the ground when she ran to get help. Reyna had no idea how to administer CPR but she managed to do it based on what she had seen on TV. An ambulance showed up shortly and rushed the baby to the hospital.

The baby was 1-year-old Domingo. After his mom had given Domingo a bath, she pulled the plug in the bathtub and searched for some baby wash under the sink. When she returned to the tub the baby was not breathing.

You may be wondering how Hunter sensed that the baby was in danger. The police who responded to the scene provided the answer. It turns out that Hunter had been trained in child rescue. Unfortunately, he did not pass the necessary tests and was dismissed from the program. Even though Hunter never made the final cut, he never forgot what he learned during his training.

Reyna never knew that her dog had this ability. Domingo's mom is so thankful that Hunter came to the rescue. Domingo was treated and released from the hospital in great condition.

This story could have had a very tragic ending but heroic Hunter saved the day.

<u>Mabeline</u>

Many times, shelters utilize volunteers to help walk dogs and take care of them. The Friends of Strays Animal Shelter in St. Petersburg, Florida eagerly accepts volunteers. The shelter needs as much help as possible caring for the animals.

One day, a 12-year-old female volunteer was walking a dog named Mabeline. Mabeline is a Rhodesian Ridgeback Mix. She was found wandering the streets of St. Petersburg and taken to the shelter to be cared for. While Mabeline was enjoying her walk with the young volunteer, an attacker came up from behind. The attacker grabbed the girl by the hair and forced her to the ground.

Mabeline quickly came to the girl's aid. Mabeline was able to scare away the attacker and the girl escaped unharmed. Mabeline only weighs 38-pounds, but she gave the attacker a run for his money and saved the young girl from being harmed.

After her heroic act Mabeline was adopted by a family. Her new owner, Mary, was not aware that she had adopted a hero. When Mary was told the story months later about Mabeline's protectiveness and heroism, Mary saw Mabeline as a hero, not just the family pet.

Hercules

Lee and Elizabeth Littler could be called heroes for rescuing Hercules from a shelter that is known to euthanize dogs that are not adopted. Hercules was a very large St. Bernard who won their hearts. As big as he was when they first saw him, he was seventy-five percent underweight and looked very beaten down. He undoubtedly endured a lot of hardship before finding his way to the shelter.

Lee knew right away that this dog needed a good home. The Littlers decided to adopt him. Hercules had been very well mannered all the way home. He did not make a sound. The Littlers unloaded him from the car and unlocked the front door. Hercules immediately began to bark. Lee knew that there was something wrong because Hercules was very upset.

Hercules broke free from his leash. He crashed through the screen door and onto the back porch. Hercules leapt from the porch and raced after a man running towards the fence. The man had been trying to break into the Littler's home through the basement door. As the intruder tried to climb the fence, Hercules clamped down on the man's ankle. The intruder managed to break free from Hercules grip and get away.

It is simply amazing that the Littlers had Hercules for less than 6 hours yet he was already defending his home. He is a true hero and the Littlers made sure he got a hero's reward by giving him a bone, a spot on the bed and a permanent loving home.

This truly is a happy ending for a dog that was severely underweight and was once on death row. He was given a second chance and proved he deserved it!

<u>Danny</u>

A fall can cause a lot of injuries especially if the victim is elderly. Glendale, Arizona native Bethe Bennett provides a foster home for dogs. She is also an author and enjoys writing stories about her experiences with the dogs. Bethe has always been very fond of animals and that is why she decided to foster dogs. She believes that everyone needs a second chance and that rang true for the dogs who visited her home.

Bethe was fostering a service dog named Danny who is a miniature Schnauzer. While walking through her home, Bethe lost her footing on her tile floor and took a nasty fall. The fall left her unable to move because she had broken her thigh bone. Bethe was in a lot of pain. She was also worried that no one would find her for days. She lived alone and was not expecting company for four days.

Danny quickly came to her aid. He knocked the telephone off the hook and pushed it to Bethe. Bethe then commanded Danny to bring her a piece of paper and Danny fetched 5 pieces of paper including one that contained a neighbor's phone number. Bethe was able to call 911 then she began to alert neighbors who could produce a spare key for the medics to enter her home. The rescue team arrived at her home quickly and rushed her to the local hospital.

Thanks to Danny, Bethe received the quick medical attention that she needed. Had he not been there to help her she could have been trapped there in pain for days. Bethe is very thankful that Danny was there to rescue her. He now has a permanent

home with her.

<u>Bear</u>

Bear is a beautiful 180-pound German shepherd who lives with Deborah Zeisler in Milsap, Texas. Deborah has suffered from seizures for years and somehow Bear, who had no previous training, knows how to help her when she experiences the seizures.

Bear insists Deborah sit down and take her meds when he senses that a seizure is coming. Deborah can even ask Bear to retrieve her medicine for her. Deborah is so thankful to have Bear to watch over her. She typically always listens to Bear when he insists she sit down, but on one particular day she did not.

On that day, Deborah didn't sit down like Bear wanted. Instead, Deborah made her way out the front door and collapsed. She hit her head on a step and laid lifelessly in the front yard.

Bear came to her aid and tried to wake her. When he saw that she was not waking up, he ran to the neighbor's house and began scratching on the door. When Bear realized no one was home, he made his way on each house down the block and started scratching their neighbors' doors. Little did he know that two animal control officers were on his block taking care of a call they received. The officers saw Bear going from door to door. When Bear saw no one was going to answer at one house, he would go to the next house.

Karen Kessler, the supervisor of Parker County Animal Control, opened the door to her truck. Bear quickly jumped in and crawled in her lap. Karen noticed that Bear had two tags on his collar. One read, *I am a service dog*, and the other side said, *I am a seizure dog*. The officers were aware that service dogs do not leave their owner's side unless there is a problem.

The address on the tag was old so the officers decided to follow Bear, knowing he would lead them to his owner. When officers found Deborah, she was disoriented and confused. They called an ambulance. Bear refused to let Deborah out of his sight. He jumped into the ambulance and rode with her to the hospital.

This was not the first time Bear went to the neighbors' houses looking for help. One other time, he did the same in the middle of the night to ask for help because Deborah was also in danger. Deborah believes that Bear is her angel and that everything happens for a reason.

Have you read Jennifer Ogden's first book of dog stories?

Hero Dog Stories 1: 16 True Stories of Amazing Dogs has 16 new and different stories of heroic and amazing dogs. It's the book that launched the series! Get it today.

Recommended Books about Dogs

Here are some more great books about dogs that you may like:

Because of Winn Dixie by Kate DiCamillo

Shiloh by Phyllis Reynolds Naylor

Racing in the Rain by Garth Stein

If Only I Could Talk: A Canine Adventure by Tony Lewis

Ribsy by Beverly Cleary

Lucky Phoo by Stacia Deutsch and Rhody Cohon

Made in the USA
Middletown, DE
10 February 2019